Thank you so much for choosing our activity b
We truly hope that our book brings joy and lea

We would be honored if you could spare a moment to leave a review of our book. Your feedback is invaluable to us and helps us improve and reach more families in need of educational and entertaining resources.

Thank you again for choosing our activity book, and we can't wait to hear what you and your kids think!

MW00897913

This Book Belongs To

_____

_____

1

Welcome

To the

Ballerina Activity Book For girls Ages 6-8!

A magical world of ballet, where dreams come to life and graceful dancers fill the stage! Get ready to twirl, leap, and have lots of fun with this Ballerina Activity Book made just for you. From exciting mazes to beautiful coloring pages, from word searches to designing your own tutu, this book is filled with endless joy and exploration. So put on your ballet shoes, grab your favorite colored pencils and let's dance into a world of creativity and joy!

Let's begin this magical journey together!

Word Search #1

Get your eyes and brains ready, because it's time to search for hidden words related to Ballet! Can you find them all?

```
Y  Z  N  S  U  B  O  P  N  S  M
V  I  V  D  X  X  L  O  N  U  P
A  D  B  A  L  L  E  R  I  N  A
B  A  P  P  L  A  U  S  E  U  S
Q  A  V  M  S  H  H  S  L  V  D
N  Q  L  D  H  Y  R  J  E  B  E
P  T  O  L  O  A  T  M  G  C  D
D  A  N  C  E  R  U  E  A  Y  E
R  O  Y  H  S  T  T  Y  N  L  U
U  K  E  P  I  Q  U  E  C  D  X
J  R  I  B  B  O  N  U  E  Y  U
```

Ballet	Tutu	Dancer
Tendu	Ribbon	Applause
Shoes	Ballerina	Pique
Pas De Deux	Elegance	Rehearse

Connect the Dots #1

Let's start at the number 1 and connect it to the next number in order. Keep going until you finish the drawing

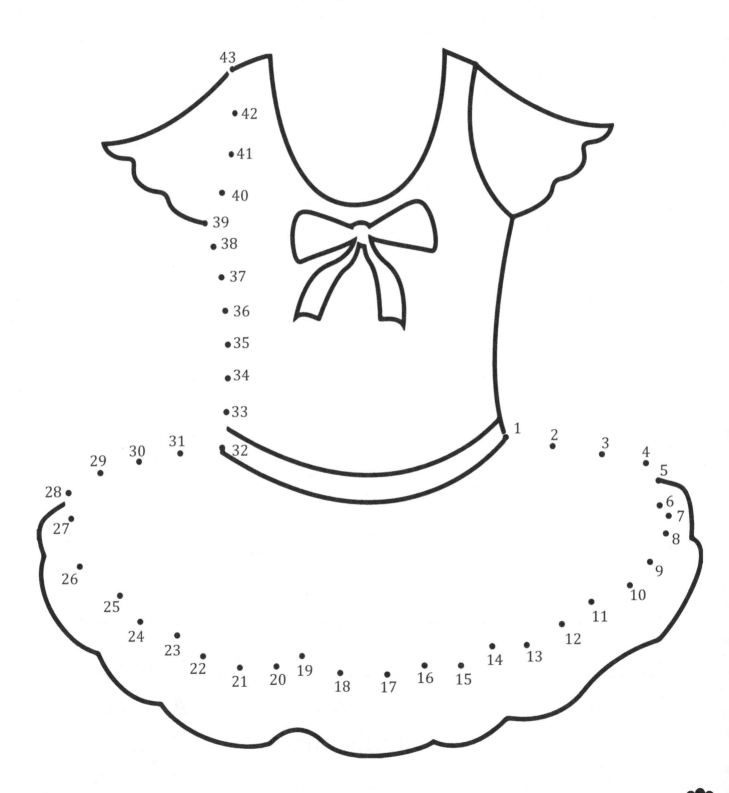

Jenny's Ballet Shoe Quest

Jenny's ballet shoes are missing, can you help her navigate the maze and find them!

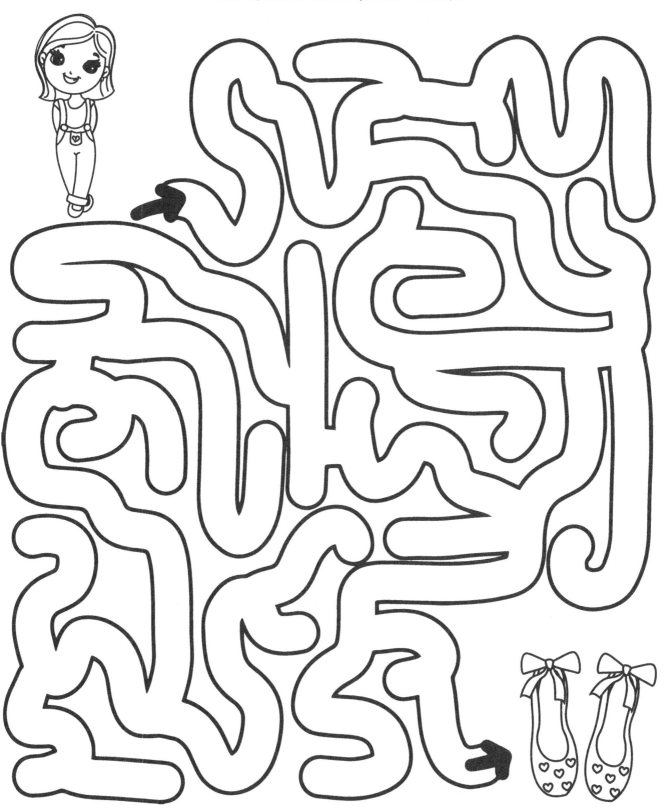

Things I Like About Ballet

Can You Share Five Things You Love or Admire About ballet?

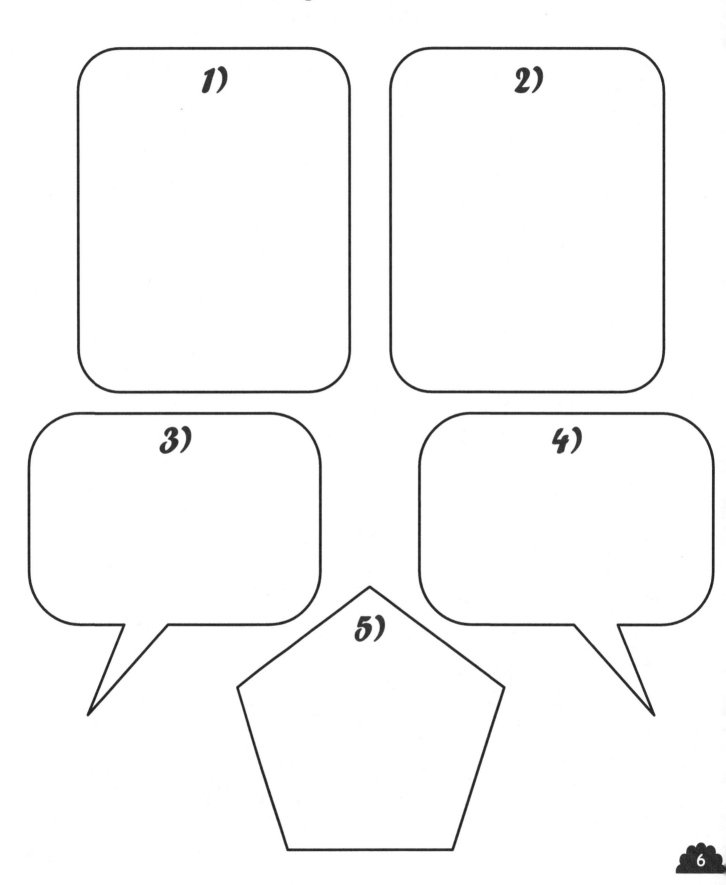

1)

2)

3)

4)

5)

Drawing Activity

Put your artistic talents to use by replicating the image with your own drawing skills

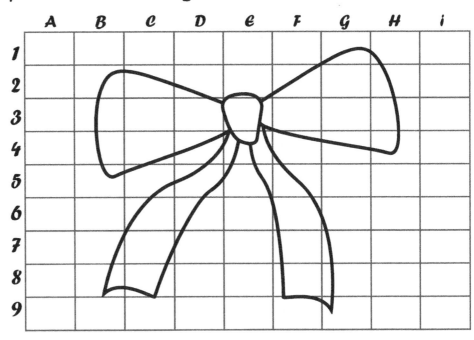

Lost and Found

Embark on an exciting adventure with Sarah as she searches for her lost crown! Follow the numbered path from 1 to 20 to help her find her crown

1	4	5	6	7
1	2	3	8	5
1	2	4	3	8	9	10
9	7	5	6	7	10	3
3	10	1	8	5	11	7
4	2	12	14	13	12	2
12	13	16	15	11	16	19
15	9	17	4	5		
16	10	18	19	20		

Spot the Perfect Match #1

Can you match the ballet dancers with their correct match

11

I Can Write

Say it and spell it

Ballerina

Trace it and Write it

Tutu Design

Let Your Inner Designer Shine! Design and Create
Your Own One-of-a-Kind Tutu!

Word Search #2

Get your eyes and brains ready, because it's time to search for hidden words related to Ballet! Can you find them all?

```
V T M U Q Q J Y M B O
D K Z O Z A I A C L L
L O Y F O W B P Z P Y
R O Y Y C L A S S O E
M O S U C U R T A I N
Q P A T T E R N R N V
S T A G E K E L E T X
X R F R E V E A L E K
G R A C E Q V X E N O
G C H A I N E S V J H
X W L C M J E T E I M
```

Chaines	Releve	Jete
Stage	Grace	Barre
Class	Pattern	Pointe
Career	Reveal	Curtain

15

Maze Challenge

This ballerina has lost her water bottle. it's really important to remain hydrated when we exercise so can you help her find her way through the maze to her bottle

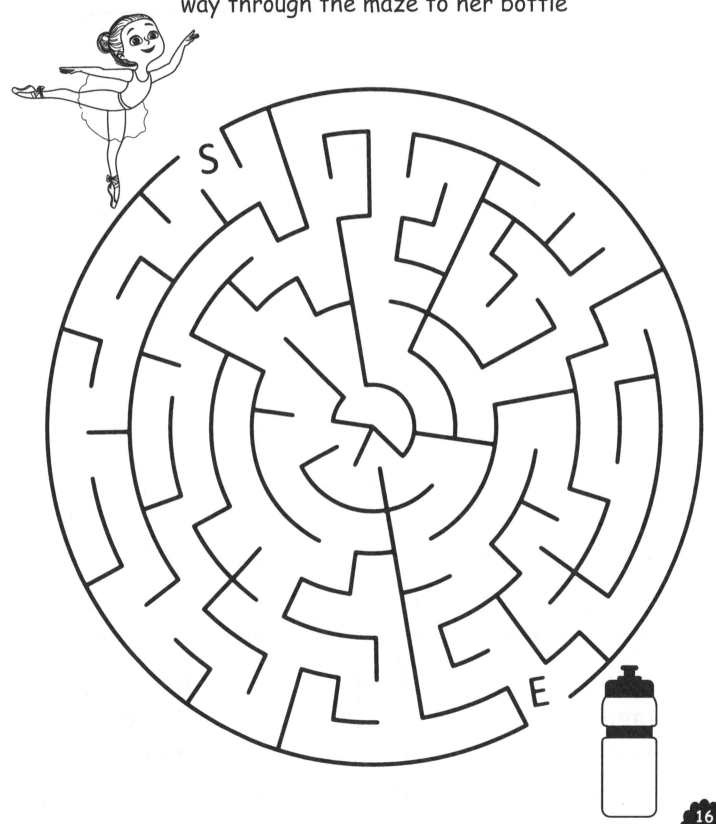

Magical Makeup

Unleash Your inner makeup artist and Design a Beautiful Makeup Look for the Ballerina!

Crossword Game #1

Word Bank

Port de bras
Ballet shoes
Barre
First position
Solo
Sauté
Pirouette
Plie
french
Ballet

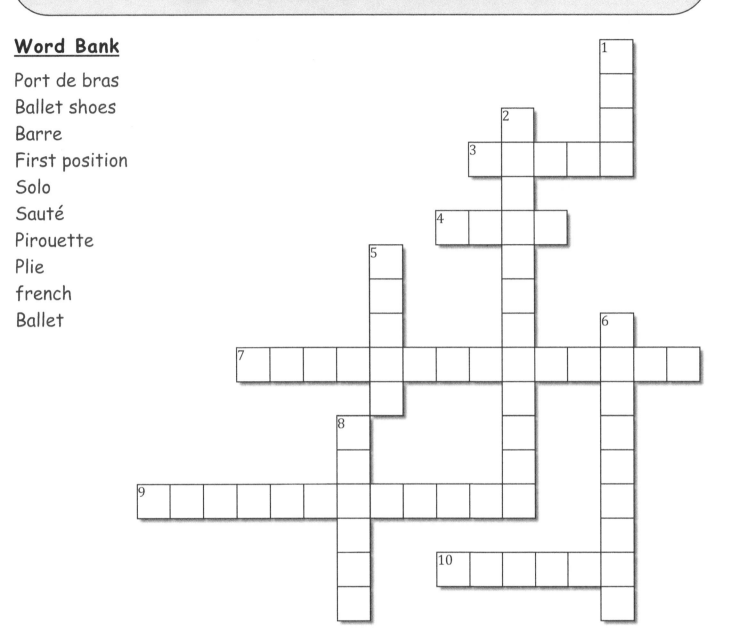

Across

3. A wooden rod used by dancers for support during practice

4. A performance by a single dancer or a duet

7. The position where heels are touching and toes are turned out

9. The basic ballet position where the arms are rounded and curved.

10. The graceful dance form that tells stories through movement

Down

1. The ballet movement where a dancer bends

their knees while keeping their heels on the ground.

2. The footwear that ballet dancers wear

5. A small, light step where a dancer jumps from one foot to the other.

6. The movement where a dancer spins on one leg

8. What language is ballet taught in?

Ballet Scramble Game

Unscramble the Names of Ballet Items and Put Your Ballet Knowledge to the Test!

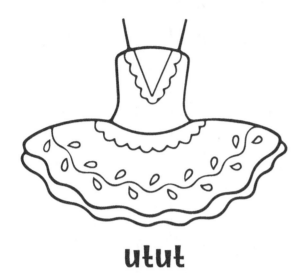

utut

aitar

rikts

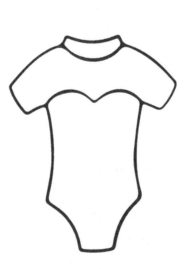

dlarote

soehs

Odd and Even Numbers

Let's find the Tiaras with even numbers!
Can you cercle them all?

Connect the Dots #2

Let's start at the number 1 and connect it to the next number in order. Keep going until you finish the drawing

24

Ballet Words Matching #1

Connect the Ballet Words to Their Meanings by Drawing a Line

Plié	to disengage
Relevé	to glide
Tendu	to beat
Glissade	to bend
Sauté	to rise
Battement	to stretch
Degage	to jump

Tiara Counting Activity

Let's count together! Keep track of the tiaras and fill in the blanks

👑 👑 👑 + 👑 👑 = ☐

👑 + = 2

👑 👑 + 👑 👑 👑 👑 👑 👑 = ☐

👑 👑 👑 👑 + = 9

👑 + 👑 👑 👑 = ☐

👑 👑 👑 + 👑 👑 👑 = ☐

👑 👑 👑 👑 + = 8

👑 + 👑 👑 = ☐

Accessorize The Hand

Let's spark some creativity! Accessorize the ballerina's hand with your unique style

In 20 Years ...

Imagine yourself 20 years in the future, as a wonderful ballerina!
Complete the sentences below to share your dreams and goals.
Fill in the blanks with your ideas and dreams.
Have fun dreaming big and let your imagination soar!

By: _____

When I'm older, I want to dance on a big stage called _____.

I will practice my favorite ballet move called _____, and I'll be really good at it!

I will wear beautiful costumes with sparkly _____ on them.

As a famous ballerina, I will travel to perform in different countries like _____.

Other kids will look up to me and say, "Wow, you dance so _____!"

In 20 years, I will dance with a famous ballet company called _____.

I will win special awards for my amazing _____ in ballet.

When I dance, I will express my feelings and tell stories with my _____ moves.

In the future, I will be known as a fantastic _____ all around the world

Word Search #3

Get your eyes and brains ready, because it's time to search for hidden words related to Ballet! Can you find them all?

```
U  W  N  J  H  Y  Z  D  B  W  H
F  S  N  Z  U  E  O  J  E  C  S
W  O  X  C  A  T  C  H  U  M  L
E  G  U  D  R  L  H  B  F  M  I
D  N  R  E  A  D  A  G  I  O  P
B  N  C  C  T  L  S  R  Y  I  P
W  D  S  O  H  T  S  H  L  L  E
U  X  G  R  R  X  E  F  P  P  R
P  A  R  T  N  E  R  N  W  I  B
Y  A  U  D  I  E  N  C  E  H  S
A  J  T  J  W  J  V  H  G  Q  W
```

Fouette	Demi	Catch
Adagio	Audience	Encore
Partner	Jump	Decor
Slipper	Chasse	Flip

Leotard Design

Let Your Inner Designer Shine! Design and Create
Your Own One-of-a-Kind Leotard!

I Can Write

Say it and spell it

Tiara

Trace it and Write it

Crossword Game #2

Word Bank

Tutu
Score
Fouette
Pointe
Developpe
Pianist
Auditorium
Assemble
Grand jete

Across

3. The part of the ballet theater where the audience sits

4. A long, sustained stretch where a dancer extends one leg in the air.

7. A jump where a dancer brings legs together in the air and lands on both feet.

8. The costume worn by a ballet dancer

9. The piece of music that accompanies a ballet performance.

Down

1. A ballet movement where a dancer jumps and kicks their legs in the air

2. The person who accompanies ballet dancers on the piano.

5. The movement where a dancer stands on the tips of their toes.

6. A graceful turn where a dancer rotates on the tips of their toes

My Dream Ballet Costume

Draw a picture of your dream ballet costume.
What colors and designs would you include?

Math Crown

Put your math skills to the test by solving these two-digit addition problems, using regrouping if needed

23
+ 35
___

47
+ 15
___

26
+ 30
___

18
+ 18
___

59
+ 20
___

88
+ 11
___

37
+ 22
___

55
+ 44
___

17
+ 65
___

75
+ 15
___

12
+ 16
___

31
+ 32
___

Ballerinas Name

Put your ballet knowledge to the test! How many Ballerinas can you name?

1. _ _ _ _ _ _ _ _ _ _ _ _ _ _ _ _ _ _ _   2. _ _ _ _ _ _ _ _ _ _ _ _ _ _ _ _ _ _ _

3. _ _ _ _ _ _ _ _ _ _ _ _ _ _ _ _ _ _   4. _ _ _ _ _ _ _ _ _ _ _ _ _ _ _ _ _ _ _

5. _ _ _ _ _ _ _ _ _ _ _ _ _ _ _ _ _   6. _ _ _ _ _ _ _ _ _ _ _ _ _ _ _ _ _ _ _

7. _ _ _ _ _ _ _ _ _ _ _ _ _ _ _ _ _   8. _ _ _ _ _ _ _ _ _ _ _ _ _ _ _ _ _ _ _

9. _ _ _ _ _ _ _ _ _ _ _ _ _ _ _ _ _   10. _ _ _ _ _ _ _ _ _ _ _ _ _ _ _ _ _ _

11. _ _ _ _ _ _ _ _ _ _ _ _ _ _ _ _ _   12. _ _ _ _ _ _ _ _ _ _ _ _ _ _ _ _ _ _

13. _ _ _ _ _ _ _ _ _ _ _ _ _ _ _ _ _   14. _ _ _ _ _ _ _ _ _ _ _ _ _ _ _ _ _ _

15. _ _ _ _ _ _ _ _ _ _ _ _ _ _ _ _ _   16. _ _ _ _ _ _ _ _ _ _ _ _ _ _ _ _ _ _

17. _ _ _ _ _ _ _ _ _ _ _ _ _ _ _ _ _   18. _ _ _ _ _ _ _ _ _ _ _ _ _ _ _ _ _ _

19. _ _ _ _ _ _ _ _ _ _ _ _ _ _ _ _ _   20. _ _ _ _ _ _ _ _ _ _ _ _ _ _ _ _ _ _

Drawing Activity

Put your artistic talents to use by replicating the image with your own drawing skills

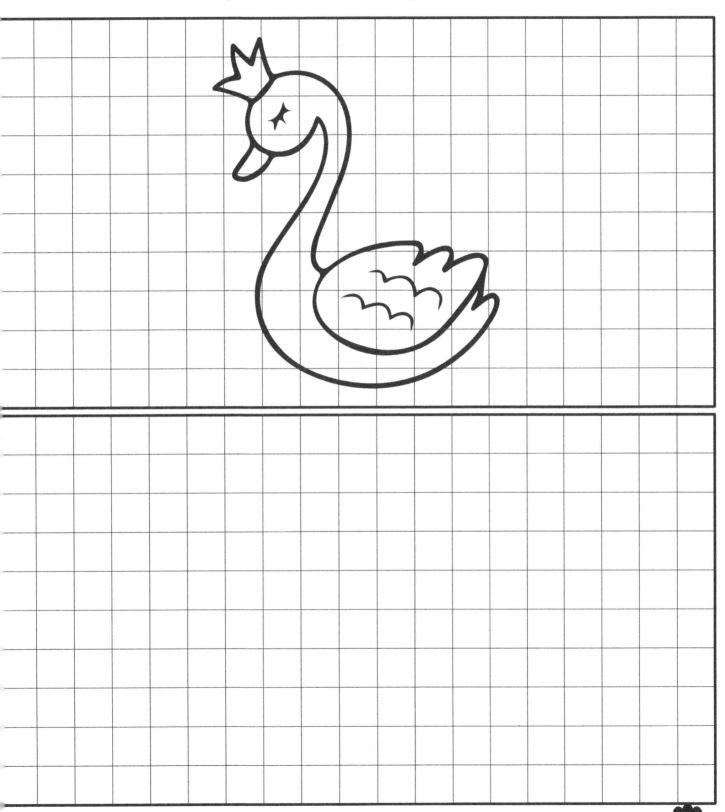

Lily's Lost Tiara

Lily, the ballerina, has misplaced her precious tiara! Can you lend a hand and guide her through the maze to find it.

Magical Ballet Accessory

Imagine you have a magical ballet accessory.
Draw it and Describe Its Special Powers!

Ballet Words Matching #2

Connect the Ballet Words to Their Meanings by Drawing a Line

Adagio	to strike
Allongé	separated
Ballon	whipped
Chassé	to extended
Fouetté	to bounce
Écarté	slow tempo
Frappé	to chase

Spot the Perfect Match #2

Can you match the ballet dancers with their correct match

Drawing Activity

Mirror the image! Finish the right side of the picture by copying the lines from the left side

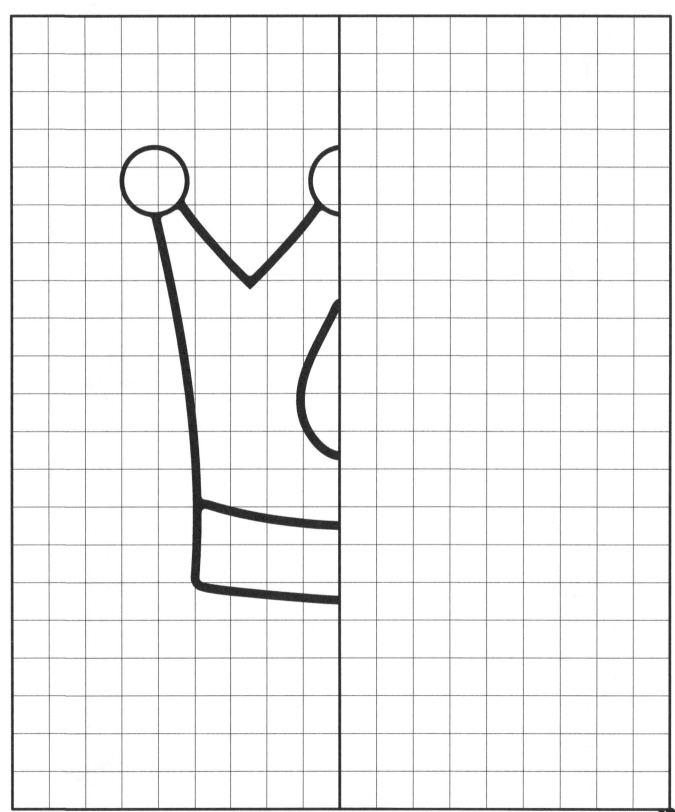

Ballet Smoothie Creations

Ballerinas need lots of energy to fuel their graceful dancing!
In this activity, let your imagination run wild as you create
a refreshing and nutritious ballet-inspired smoothie.
Decorate the cup to showcase your smoothie creation!

Name of the Smoothie: _____

Ingredients Needed:

Math Maze

Time to show off your math skills! Help Emma find her skirt by coloring only the circles that have even numbers inside!

54 x 5 =

37 x 3 =

85 x 7 =

53 x 9 =

26 x 6 =

86 x 9 =

48 x 2 =

27 x 7 =

87 x 3 =

79 x 5 =

37 x 8 =

88 x 7 =

75 x 6 =

64 x 4 =

98 x 3 =

96 x 5 =

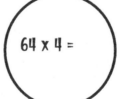
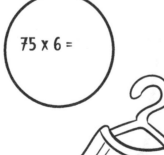

47 x 9 =

Word Search #4

Get your eyes and brains ready, because it's time to search for hidden words related to Ballet! Can you find them all?

```
V A R I A T I O N G J
U R O E G Y S C W Q E
Z P T P C T L Y E D E
S I A L H I T T U D F
L K T G O F T T N E R
P L I E T E I A H M V
Z T O P U T R C L D O
L M N O T G N D X T R
P A R A B E S Q U E W
V I L O P C R E A T E
P O Q C D T A A L U W
```

Skip	Pirouette	Tights
Arabesque	Variation	Penche
Create	Grande	Rotation
Recital	Plie	Attitude

Connect the Dots #3

Let's start at the number 1 and connect it to the next number in order. Keep going until you finish the drawing

Crossword Game #3

Word Bank

Tendu
Dance belt
attitude
Tiara
Petit saut
Leg warmers
Leotard
Dresser
Arabesque
Ribbons

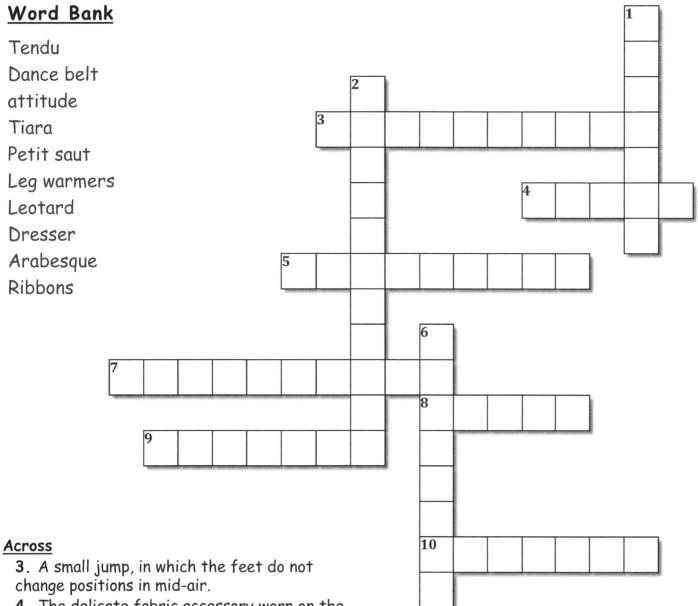

Across

3. A small jump, in which the feet do not change positions in mid-air.

4. The delicate fabric accessory worn on the head of a ballerina, often adorned with jewels or feathers.

5. A ballet movement where a dancer stands on one leg with the other leg extended behind.

7. The elegant accessory worn around the waist of a ballerina to accentuate the movements

8. Ballet step where the foot stretches and slides along the floor.

9. The fabric that secures and ties the ballet shoes onto a dancer's feet

10. The person who helps ballet dancers with their costumes and makeup.

Down

1. A piece of clothing that covers a ballerina's torso and is often decorated with sequins or lace.

2. The soft, stretchy leg coverings worn by dancers to keep the muscles warm and protected.

6. A ballet exercise where a dancer balances on one leg with the other leg bent

I Can Write

Say it and spell it

Leotard

Trace it and Write it

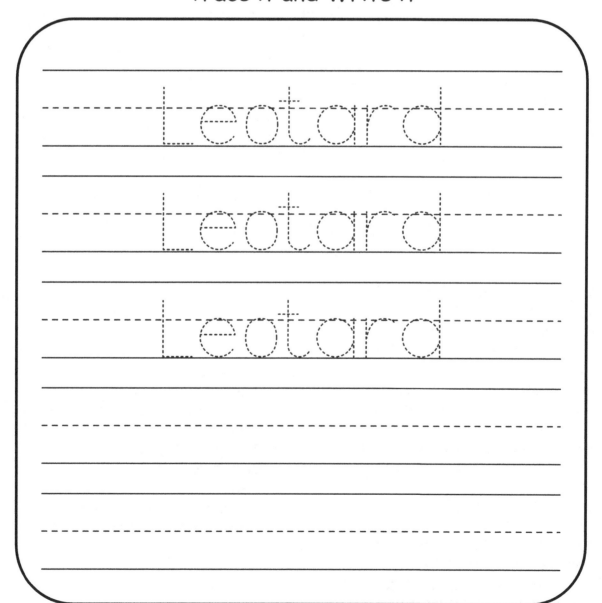

Ballet Math Puzzle

Can you solve the puzzle

$$\text{(arms up)} = 2 \qquad \text{(standing)} = 3 \qquad \text{(dancing)} = 5$$

arms up + dancing + standing + arms up = ☐

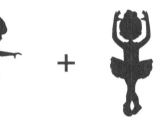

dancing + dancing + standing = ☐

standing + arms up + dancing + dancing + arms up = ☐

arms up + dancing + dancing + arms up = ☐

Find the Dance Partner!

Help the Ballerina Find Her Dance Partner!
Solve the Maze and Showcase Your Problem-Solving Skills!

Design a Tiara

Design a special and sparkly tiara that you can wear when you become a graceful ballerina performing on a big stage.

The Basic Positions

There are five basic positions of the feet that most ballet steps are based on. Draw a line to connect each footprint with its corresponding position.

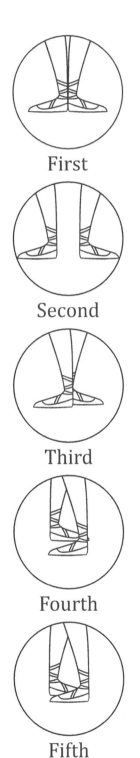

First

Second

Third

Fourth

Fifth

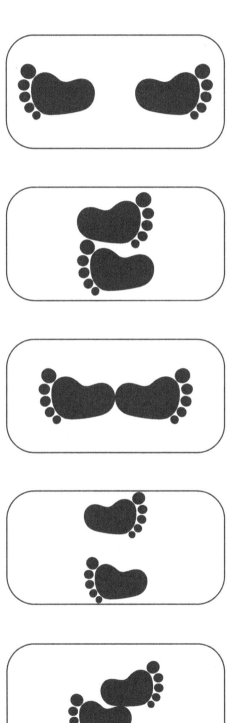

Drawing Activity

Put your artistic talents to use by replicating the image with your own drawing skills

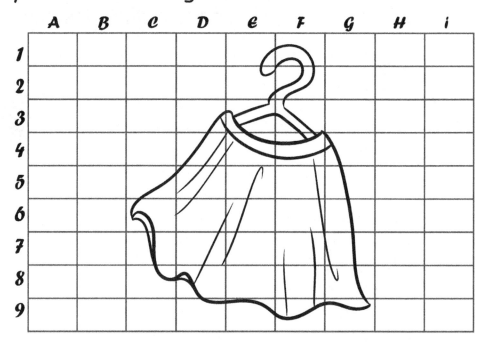

	A	B	C	D	E	F	G	H	i
1									
2									
3									
4									
5									
6									
7									
8									
9									

Word Search #5

Get your eyes and brains ready, because it's time to search for hidden words related to Ballet! Can you find them all?

```
P E R F O R M F F U S
M D P X I M N I A L B
U Y X Y R P R S I O A
P Y V F F E E T R F L
D S E O M O X G Y L L
O W V L T H E A T E R
S D G S I L R Y V X O
R P O W L V C C P U O
O E L A C T I O N E M
A A R I Z U S L U K P
P S A U T D E C H A T
```

Saut De Chat   Fairy   Theater
Ballroom   Perform Flex
Allegro   Action   Feet
Split   Exercise Toes

Math Challenge

Let's have some fun with numbers and multiplication! Use the numbers on the stars to complete the circles and create the perfect equation.

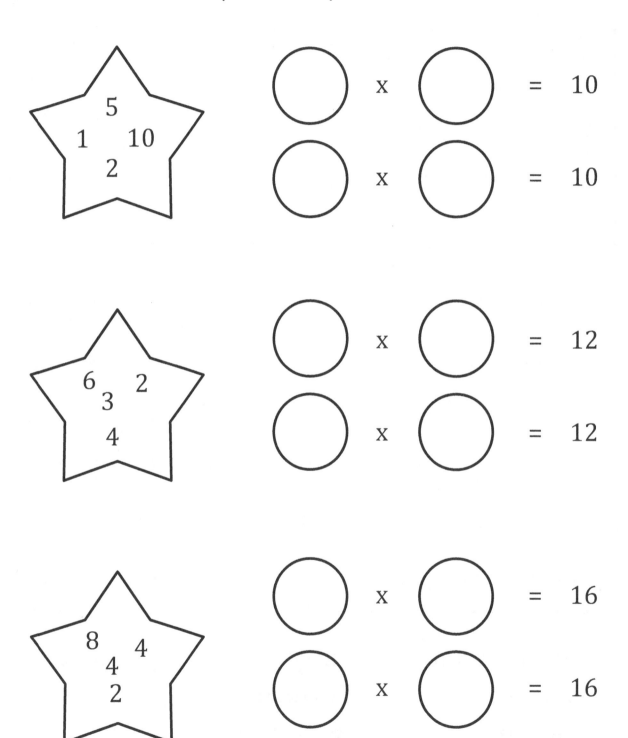

Design Your Own Ballet Shoes

Unleash Your Inner Designer! Create Your Own Unique Ballet Shoes!

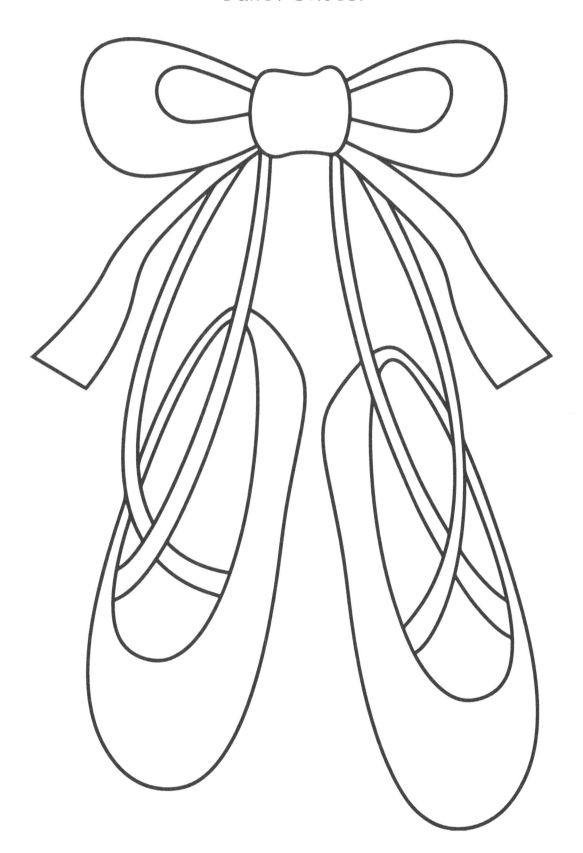

Dress Adventure!

Join the Ballerina's Dress Quest! Can You
Help Her Find the Perfect Dress?

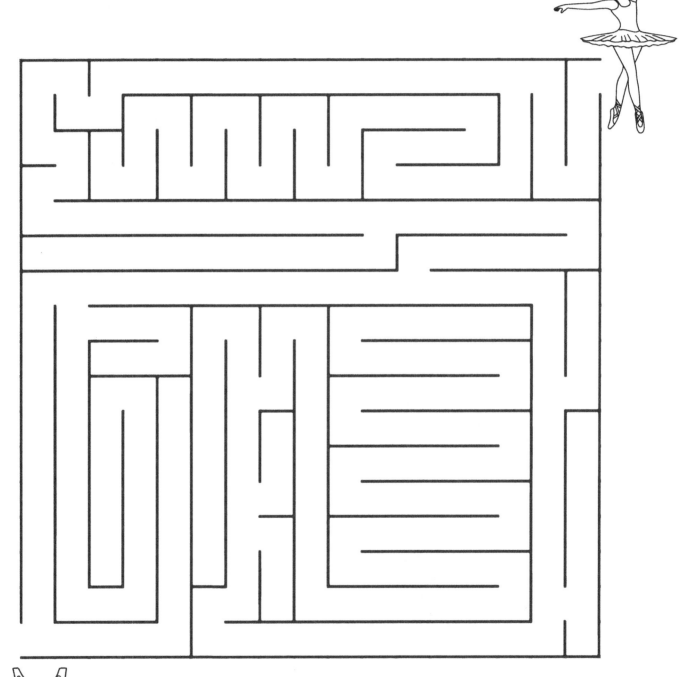

Spot The Difference

Can you find 6 differences?

Shadow Matching

Can You Find the Right Shadow? Test Your Skills and Match Them Up!

I Can Write

Say it and spell it

Dance

Trace it and Write it

Drawing Activity

Mirror the image! Finish the right side of the picture by copying the lines from the left side

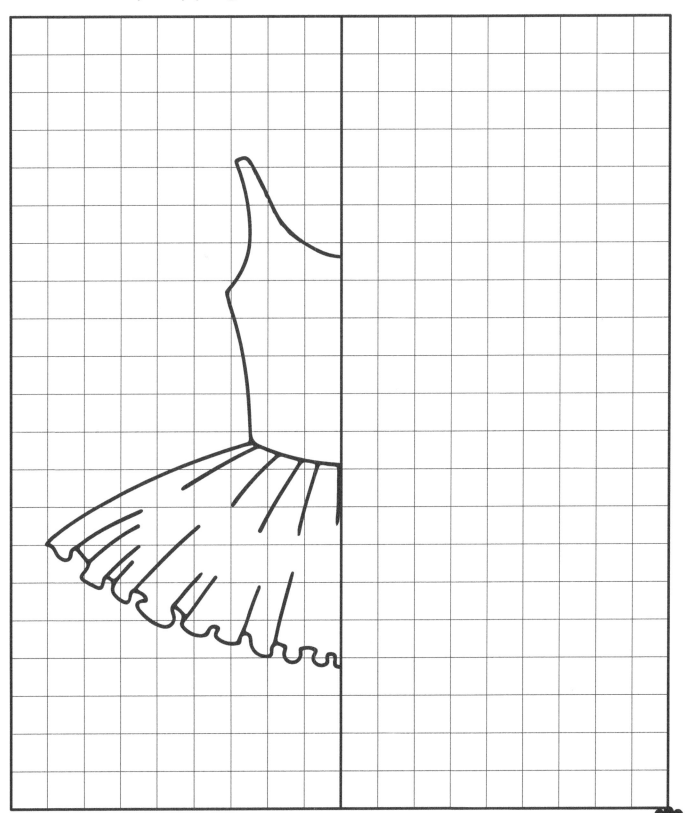

Connect the Dots #4

Let's start at the number 1 and connect it to the next number in order. Keep going until you finish the drawing

Colorful Comparison

Let's Compare Numbers with < and > and Color the Tiara with
the Bigger Number!

Find the Missing Smoothie!

Oh no! The tired ballerina is in need of her refreshing smoothie, but she can't find it anywhere. Can you lend a hand and help her find the missing smoothie?

Solutions

Word Search #1

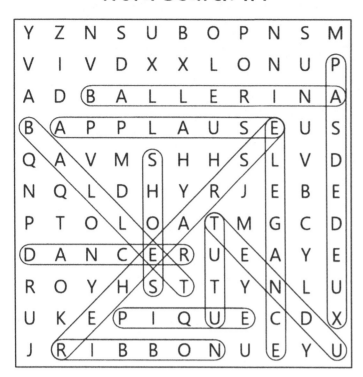

Jenny's Ballet Shoe Quest

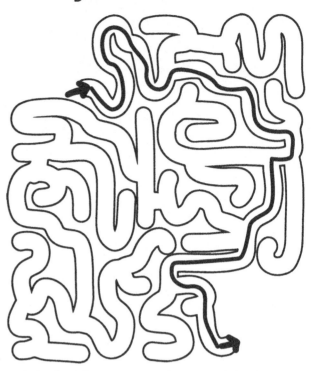

Lost and Found

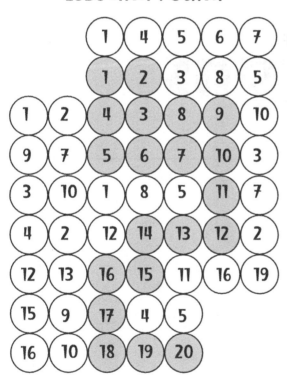

Spot the Perfect Match #1

Word Search #2

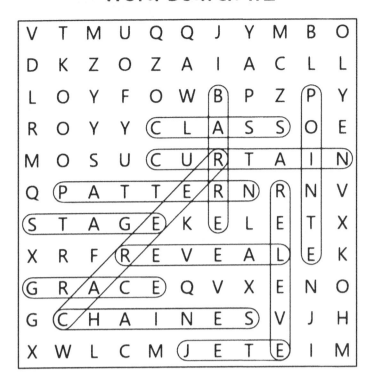

V	T	M	U	Q	Q	J	Y	M	B	O
D	K	Z	O	Z	A	I	A	C	L	L
L	O	Y	F	O	W	B	P	Z	P	Y
R	O	Y	Y	C	L	A	S	S	O	E
M	O	S	U	C	U	R	T	A	I	N
Q	P	A	T	T	E	R	N	R	N	V
S	T	A	G	E	K	E	L	E	T	X
X	R	F	R	E	V	E	A	L	E	K
G	R	A	C	E	Q	V	X	E	N	O
G	C	H	A	I	N	E	S	V	J	H
X	W	L	C	M	J	E	T	E	I	M

Maze Challenge

Crossword Game #1

1. p l i e (down)
2. b (down)
3. b a r r e (across)
4. s o l o (across)
5. s a u t é (down)
6. p i r o u e t t e (down)
7. f i r s t p o s i t i o n (across)
8. f r e n c h (down)
9. p o r t d e b r a s (across)
10. b a l l e t e (across)

Ballet Scramble Game

utut = tutu
dlarote = leotard
soehs = shoes
aitar = tiara
rikts = Skirt

Ballet Words Matching #1

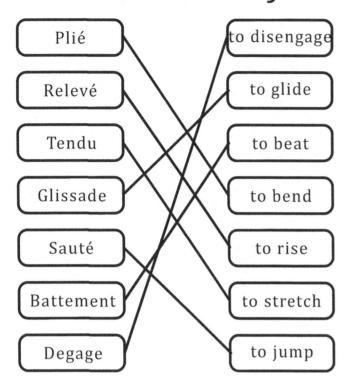

Plié	to disengage
Relevé	to glide
Tendu	to beat
Glissade	to bend
Sauté	to rise
Battement	to stretch
Degage	to jump

Cloud Counting Activity

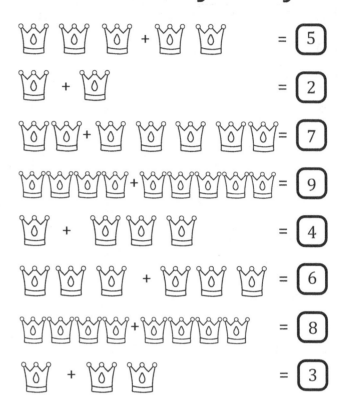

= 5
= 2
= 7
= 9
= 4
= 6
= 8
= 3

Word Search #3

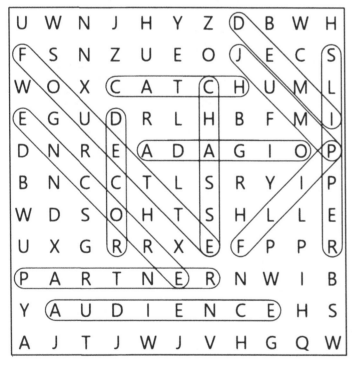

```
U W N J H Y Z D B W H
F S N Z U E O J E C S
W O X C A T C H U M L
E G U D R L H B F M I
D N R E A D A G I O P
B N C C T L S R Y I P
W D S O H T S H L L E
U X G R R X E F P P R
P A R T N E R N W I B
Y A U D I E N C E H S
A J T J W J V H G Q W
```

Crossword Game #2

1 g r
2 p i a n i s t e
3 a u d i t o r i u m
a n j t e
4 d e v e l o p p e
5 p o i n
6 f
7 a s s e m b l e
8 t u t u
9 s c o r e
o u e t t é

Math Crown

$$\begin{array}{r} 23 \\ + 35 \\ \hline 58 \end{array}$$ $$\begin{array}{r} 47 \\ + 15 \\ \hline 62 \end{array}$$ $$\begin{array}{r} 26 \\ + 30 \\ \hline 56 \end{array}$$

$$\begin{array}{r} 18 \\ + 18 \\ \hline 36 \end{array}$$ $$\begin{array}{r} 59 \\ + 20 \\ \hline 79 \end{array}$$ $$\begin{array}{r} 88 \\ + 11 \\ \hline 99 \end{array}$$

$$\begin{array}{r} 37 \\ + 22 \\ \hline 59 \end{array}$$ $$\begin{array}{r} 55 \\ + 44 \\ \hline 99 \end{array}$$ $$\begin{array}{r} 17 \\ + 65 \\ \hline 82 \end{array}$$

$$\begin{array}{r} 75 \\ + 15 \\ \hline 90 \end{array}$$ $$\begin{array}{r} 12 \\ + 16 \\ \hline 28 \end{array}$$ $$\begin{array}{r} 31 \\ + 32 \\ \hline 63 \end{array}$$

Lily's Lost Tiara

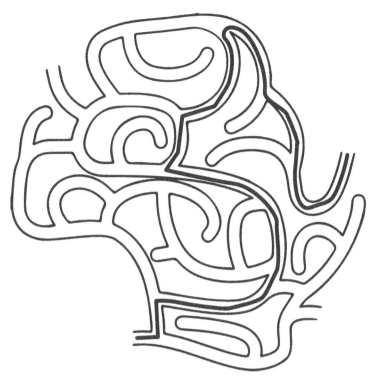

Ballet Words Matching #2

Adagio	to strike
Allongé	separated
Ballon	whipped
Chassé	to extended
Fouetté	to bounce
Écarté	slow tempo
Frappé	to chase

Spot the Perfect Match #2

79

Math Maze

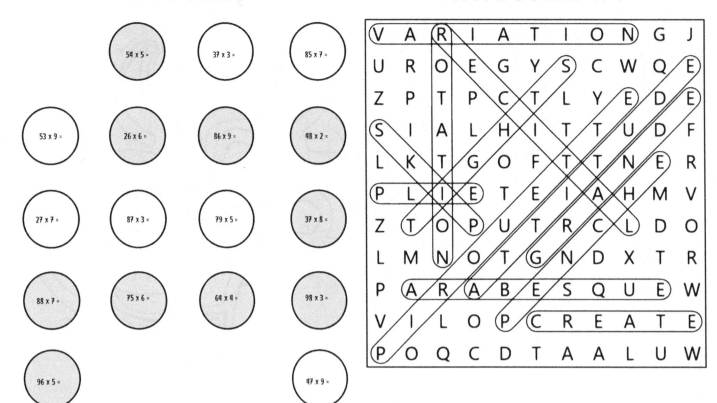

Word Search #4

Crossword Game #3

Ballet Math Puzzle

(silhouette) + (silhouette) + (silhouette) + (silhouette) = [12]

(silhouette) + (silhouette) + (silhouette) = [13]

(silhouette) + (silhouette) + (silhouette) + (silhouette) + (silhouette) = [16]

(silhouette) + (silhouette) + (silhouette) + (silhouette) + (silhouette) = [17]

(silhouette) + (silhouette) + (silhouette) + (silhouette) = [14]

Find the Dance Partner!

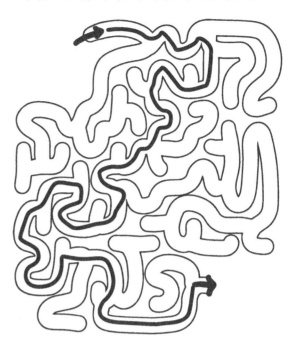

The Basic Positions

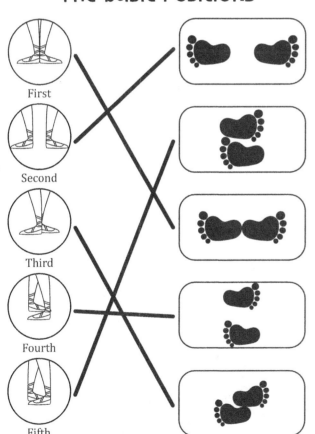

First

Second

Third

Fourth

Fifth

Word Search #5

```
P E R F O R M  F  F  U  S
M D P X I M N I A L B
U Y X Y R P R S I O A
P Y V F E E T R R F L
D S E O M O X G Y L L
O W V L T H E A T E R
S D G S I L R Y V X O
R P O W L V C C P U O
O E L A C T I O N E M
A A R I Z U S L U K P
P S A U T D E C H A T
```

Math Challenge

(10) x (1) = 10

(5) x (2) = 10

(6) x (2) = 12

(3) x (4) = 12

(8) x (2) = 16

(4) x (4) = 16

Dress Adventure!

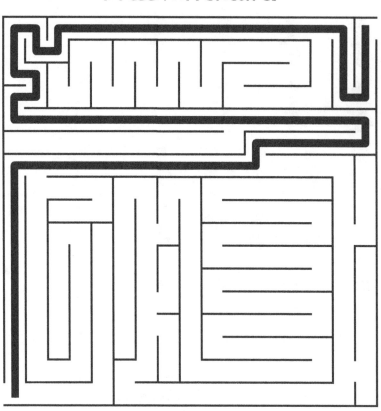

Colorful Comparison

56 < 75	18 < 25
109 < 124	16 > 11
29 > 18	92 < 99
54 > 45	44 < 89
73 < 93	15 > 13

Find the Missing Smoothie!

Thank you for purchasing our activity book for kids!

We hope your child had fun completing the activities and that the book brought a little bit of fun and creativity into their day.

If you have a moment, we would really appreciate it if you could leave a review on Amazon. Your feedback helps other parents decide if the book is right for their children, and it helps us improve and reach more families in need of educational and entertaining resources. Plus, it's always nice to hear what people think of our work!

Thank you in advance for your help, and we hope you and your child have a great day!

Kindest regards,

Creative Funland

Made in the USA
Monee, IL
01 December 2024

71824806R10046